MW01222450

The Fear of Hell Restrains Men from Sin

by

Solomon Stoddard
Pastor of the Church in
Northampton, MA

Edited by Dr. Don Kistler

Soli Deo Gloria Publications
. . . *for instruction in righteousness* . . .

Soli Deo Gloria Publications
A Division of Soli Deo Gloria Ministries, Inc.
P. O. Box 451, Morgan, PA 15064
(412) 221-1901/FAX 221-1902
www.SDGbooks.com

*

*

ISBN 1-57358-141-0

Library of Congress Cataloging-in-Publication Data

Stoddard, Solomon, 1643-1729.
  [Efficacy of the fear of hell to restrain men from sin]
  The fear of hell restrains men from sin / by Solomon Stoddard;
edited by Don Kistler.
        p. cm.
  ISBN 1-57358-141-0
  1. Hell–Christianity–Sermons. 2. Sermons, American–18th
century. 3. Congregational churches–Sermons. I. Kistler, Don.
II. Title.
BT836.3 .S76 2003
252'.3–dc21
                    2002152113

The Fear of Hell Restrains Men From Sin

"Destruction from God was a terror to me." Job 31:23

In the foregoing verses, Job makes a solemn protestation of his innocence, and, in verse 22, utters a terrible imprecation against himself in case he was guilty: "Then let mine arm fall away from my shoulder blade, and mine arm be broken from the bone." And in verse 23 he gives the reason why he did not carry himself wickedly: "Destruction from God was a terror to me."

In these words, mind (1) how Job was affected. "Terror" denotes great fear. Destruction from God was terrible to him. Also mind (2) with what he was affected: "Destruction from God." The Hebrew is literally "of God." The genitive case notes the efficient, not the subject.

QUESTION. How did Job come to be afraid of destruction from God, seeing that he was not only a good man, but, as appears by many passages in this book, he had the assurance of his salvation?

ANSWER 1. There are temporal destructions that good men are in danger of, such as the destruction of their estates, of their children, and of their lives. If they carry on rebelliously, they have no security that such destruction shall not come upon them.

ANSWER 2. Godly men have reason to be afraid of hell. Let me distinguish here that there is a slavish fear of hell rising from a sense that men are in a state of condemnation; in this way godly men should not fear hell. But there is also a cautious fear of hell that makes man avoid those paths that lead to hell; and this ought to be in godly men. That conditional proposition given in Romans 8:13 is true of godly men too: "If you live after the flesh, you shall die." And therefore godly men should have an awful fear of hell, and a due care to avoid it. Matthew 10:28: "Fear Him that can cast both soul and body into hell." It is a laudable thing for godly men to fear hell.

DOCTRINE: The fear of hell is a powerful restraint from sin. There are such strong inclinations in men to sin, and so many temptations, that the world would be more wicked than the old world were there not something that had considerable power to restrain men; and a principal thing to restrain men is the fear of hell. There are several other things that are of use to restrain men, such as the fear of the displeasure of parents, the justice of rulers, or divine vengeance in this world; but the fear of hell is much more powerful than these.

The misery of many men is that they do not fear hell; they are not sensible of the dreadfulness or danger of damnation, and so they take a great liberty to sin. But if they were afraid of hell, they would be afraid of sin. When their lusts were as spurs to stir them up to sin, this fear would be as a bridle to curb them in. Men are informed in the Scriptures of the miseries of hell on purpose to debar them from sin. Matthew 5:29–30: If thy right eye offend thee, pluck it out, and cast it from thee, for it is profitable for thee that one of thy members should perish, and not that thy whole body should be cast into hell." If men are thoroughly afraid of hell, it will have the effect of restraining them from sin.

QUESTION. How is the fear of hell a powerful restraint?

ANSWER 1. The fear of hell reveals the dangerous nature of sin. Hell is threatened in the Scripture as the punishment of sin. Matthew 13:41–42: "They shall gather out of His kingdom all things that offend, and them that do iniquity, and cast them into a furnace of fire." Sinful carriages bring destruction; hence the man is afraid of sin as that which will sink him into hell. Men are afraid of poison and the plague because they think those things will kill them; so they dread sin as that which will destroy them. Though they love it, yet they dare not practice it because of the doleful consequence of it. They say that they shall bring a curse upon themselves; they see death in it, and hereby they see an unanswerable argument against sin.

A man says, "If I should sin, I should work falsehood against my own life" (2 Samuel 18:13). This makes the temptations to sin lose their power.

Men are urged to sin for their profit, but they say, "What profit shall I have if I am damned?" Matthew 16:26: "What is a man profited if he gain the whole world and lose his own soul?"

They are urged to sin for pleasure, but they say, "We shall have pain instead of pleasure." Proverbs 5:4–5: "Her end is bitter as wormwood, sharp as a two-edged sword. Her feet go down to death; her steps take hold of hell."

They are urged to sin for their honor, but they say, "This is the way to bring ourselvees to shame." Daniel 12:2: "Some shall rise to shame and everlasting contempt."

ANSWER 2. The fear of hell helps men to see something of the baseness of sin. When men are afraid of hell, they are thereby made sensible of the terrible anger of God for sin, and may rationally conclude that sin is an exceedingly great evil. If it were not, God would not be so angry as to send men to hell on that account. Would God inflict eternal punishment for it if the evil of it were not exceedingly great? There is a great deal of light in hellfire, revealing that sin must be an abominable thing. If we should see persons burned at a stake under a righteous government, we would conclude that they had been guilty of horrendous crimes. So it is in this case.

Besides, when men are afraid of hell, that fear leads them to consider the nature of sin; it brings them into a ponderous frame of spirit, and makes them weigh things more judiciously. And when they do this, though they have only a natural conscience, yet they may perceive a great deal of filthiness in their evil carriages. They can easily discern that there is in their sinful carriages a great deal of folly, much corrupt affection and filthiness, and baseness against the light of nature. Natural conscience condemns many sins (Romans 2:15).

ANSWER 3. The fear of hell helps men to see what practices are sinful. When men are not afraid of hell, many times they don't suspect many of their sinful practices; and if they are told that those practices are evil, they stand up and justify them, pleading greatly for them. It is almost impossible to convince them; but if the terror of hell takes hold upon them, they will easily fall under the conviction that many things are amiss which formerly they saw no evil in. Conscience is enlightened and they are sensible of their danger. "Now the Word is a sharp two-edged sword" (Hebrews 4:12). They dare not give way to a cavilling spirit as before; they consider the rule more impartially than they did; they know that fig leaves and sorry pretenses and excuses will not serve their turn when God shall judge them, and they condemn such things as they justified before.

Application

USE 1. See the reason why there is so little reformation in this land. This work of reformation has been mightily clogged, and a very little matter has been effected. The country has been prosperous in other designs. There has been an endeavor to promote clothing, and it has prospered. There has been a design to promote learning and merchandise, and these have had success. But there have been great endeavors to promote reformation. Laws have been enacted, sermons have been preached, covenants have been made, but all these endeavors have had a miscarrying womb. There has not been one sin generally reformed these last twenty years. Instead of growing better and better, the country grows worse and worse. Many seem to be incorrigible and obstinate in their pride, luxury, and profaneness. The reason for it is that they are not afraid of hell. They are afraid of poverty; they are afraid of sickness, but they are not afraid of hell. That would restrain them from sinful practices. Destruction from God would be a terror to them.

Fear of punishment from men will not make the land reform. The fear of man is of considerable use. Were it not for this, the world would be far more wicked than it is. Those who don't love virtue fear punishment. Rulers are a terror to evildoers (Romans 13:4). The benefit of government in this respect is very great, but will not make the land reform because an abundance of the sins that bring down the wrath of God upon the land don't fall under the cognizance of authority. There is a great deal of pride, murmuring, worldliness, and profaning of the Sabbath that is not punishable by law. The laws of men reach more gross iniquities; but there are many transgressions that are breaches of the laws of men. Parents may fail extremely in their duty, so may officers in the church and commonwealth, yet no law takes hold of them. There may be an abundance of iniquity found by God among a people who are yet innocent in the eye of the law.

Experience of public judgments will not make men to reform. Public judgments are monitors of obedience. God speaks audibly and sensibly in them; and sometimes they have an efficacy on the consciences of men. Psalm 78:34: "When He slew them, then they sought Him." But many times the medicine is not strong enough for the disease. Judgments destroy their outward comforts, but don't destroy their sins. Cleaning a man's teeth won't cleanse away his sins (Amos 4:6). The barrenness of the land won't make them fruitful (v. 9). When they were scorched with fire from heaven, their consciences were seared (v. 11). Ten plagues were not sufficient to work upon Pharaoh. Judgments won't deliver a people from their hard hearts. Jeremiah 5:3: "Thou hast stricken them, but they have refused to receive instructions; they have made their faces harder than a rock; they have refused to return."

Sometimes judgments make people worse. Many times men are not convinced what judgments come for; and when they have passed they are soon forgotten. Men would rather bear a pretty deal than part with their sins.

Fear of shame among men will not make them reform. Sinful carriages are a shame to men. When men sin, they degrade themselves, and act beneath the dignity of their nature. Sin is unreasonable, and shows a baseness of spirit; it brings a reproach upon a people (Proverbs 14:34). And hence some particular persons are affected with it, and scorn to make themselves a reproach. They are not willing to be as the fools in Israel, and so avoid those sins that bring ignominy. But when a people have become corrupt, many sinful practices are not counted shameful. Many things that are provocations to God are vindicated; the commonness of a practice makes it to be counted lawful. Men may practice things that are provoking to God, yet live in reputation among men; they may be accounted saints; they may be advanced to places of honor. Yea, sometimes, among a corrupt people, that which is indeed a shame is accounted an honor, and they get glory therein. Philippians 3:19: "Whose glory is their shame."

A sense of mercies and deliverances will not make man reform. A corrupt people are wont to have much mercy mingled with judgment, and sometimes God gives great deliverances to them. These things should lead men to repentance, and sometimes they are greatly affected with the goodness of God. God's mercies melt their hearts, and they promise to amend their ways; but such things seldom make a people reform. After a while the pang is over and they forget the goodness of

God. Psalm 106:12: "They sang His praise, but soon forgot His works." And verse 21: "They forgot God their
Savior, that had done great things for them." The
thoughts of the deliverance grow stale after a while,
and they lose the sense of God's mercies; yea, the mercies that God bestows upon them prove to be a snare to
them. If God bestows plenty on them, they grow more
covetous; and the more they have, the more they crave.
He who loves silver will not be satisfied with silver; and
they swell with pride, forget their dependence upon
God, and think much to be controlled. "Lest I be full
and deny Thee, and say, 'Who is the Lord?' " (Proverbs
30:9). And many times they grow voluptuous and live
the lives of Epicures. Amos 6:4–6: "They lie upon beds
of ivory, and stretch themselves upon their couches,
they eat the lambs out of the flock, and calves out of the
midst of the stall; they chant to the sound of the viol,
and invent to themselves instruments of music, like
David; they drink wine in bowls, and anoint themselves
with the chief ointment."

USE 2. We see hence that it would be a great benefit
to many men if they had more of the fear of hell. It is
worthy of our observation that of all the preachers we
read of in Scripture, none was so frequent in warning
the people to avoid hell as Jesus Christ. He was often
telling them of their danger, and persuading them, if it
were possible, to avoid damnation. Sometimes He told
them that the chaff would be burned up with un-
quenchable fire; sometimes He told them that it would
be better to enter into life with one eye than, having
two eyes, to be cast into hellfire; sometimes He told
them of their being cast into a furnace of fire where
there is wailing and gnashing of teeth; sometimes He

asked the scribes how they could escape the damnation of hell; and sometimes He reminded His hearers of the sentence that will be pronounced on the wicked at the last, "Depart from Me, ye cursed, into everlasting fire, prepared for the devil and his angels" (Matthew 25:41).

From hence we may learn that the consideration of the pains of hell is singularly useful for promoting holiness; and it would be greatly beneficial to carnal men if they had more of the fear of hell. It would make them more solemn, more prayerful, more loose from worldly enjoyments, and more cautious how they behaved themselves. And it would be a great benefit to godly men if they had more of the fear of hell; for it would help them against a lukewarm and slumbering spirit, and would strengthen their hearts against many temptations that they are wont to be outbid by. Job 31:23: "Destruction from God was a terror to me."

It would be a great benefit to parents. One of the great miseries of the land is that children are not well-educated. They are bred up to work, but are not well-instructed. Parents don't teach them, warn them, govern them, or give good examples to them. Hence many children are ignorant, rude, and profane. This unfaithfulness brings many parents to eternal ruin, and their indulgence is the cause of the damnation of their children. Eli's indulgence had an influence on the destruction of Hophni and Phineas. If parents were more careful that they might not go to hell themselves, they would be more laborious in teaching their children, and in bringing them up in the nurture and admonition of the Lord. And if they were more careful that their children might not go to hell, they would not connive at their sins, or countenance them in their

worldliness and pride. They would warn them more
solemnly, restrain and govern them more thoroughly.
Proverbs 23:14: "Thou shalt beat him with the rod, and
deliver his soul from hell."

It would be a great benefit to ministers. Ministers may fail
in their duty many ways: in not convincing men of
their sins, in not setting sufficient light before them
for their conviction, in not bearing a due testimony
against their iniquities, in not searching men thoroughly as to whether they are in Jesus Christ, by allowing men to deceive themselves with false imaginations
of peace with God, by complying with the sins of the
land, or by preaching like the scribes: without authority. But if they had a sense of the dreadfulness of
damnation, and a due care of their own salvation and
the salvation of their people, they would be more thor-
ough in their work. Paul urged Timothy by this consideration in 1 Timothy 4:16, "Take heed to thyself and to
thy doctrines, continue in them, for in so doing thou
shalt both save thyself and those that hear thee."

A sense of the terror of the Lord would be a great
help to ministers. 2 Corinthians 5:11: "Knowing the ter-
rors of the Lord, we persuade men." The solemn
thoughts of this would make them careful of their
preaching as well as their example. 1 Corinthians 9:27:
"Lest by any means, when I have preached to others, I
myself should be a castaway."

It would be a great benefit to rulers. It is a rare thing that
God is provoked with a people, but the rulers have some
hand in it. Rulers may miss it many ways; when in their
private conversations they are not good examples, that
emboldens other men to transgress. They may miss it
by being backward to promote religion, whey they are

Gallio-like, not caring for those things; when they don't strengthen the hands of under-officers by not making use of their information, allowing things to drop without due examination. They may be very faulty by not punishing vice duly, having an indulgent spirit towards those who are guilty of misdemeanors; by not stating the case right unto the jury, speaking in favor of those whose case is naught, by not cutting off the occasions of sin. Where there is much temptation, there will be much provocation, by being intimate with men of vicious conduct. This is a discredit to them, a way to harden dissolute persons. It is very profitable for rulers to have a cautious fear of hell. Those who judge others must be judged; those who sit on the bench must stand at the bar; all acts of judgment must be called over again, and have a second hearing. It is good for those who sit in judgment to remember the day wherein they must appear before the judgment seat of Christ. It is good for them to ask the question found in Job 31:14: "What shall I do when God riseth up? And when He visiteth, what shall I answer Him?"

It would be a great benefit to under-officers. The work of some under-officers is to inform themselves of the breaches of law, and to give information to rulers. They may fail in their duty by neglecting to get knowledge, lest they should be counted busybodies, and by neglecting to give information either from friendship or from fear, or to prevent trouble. There are other under-officers who are to judge in civil and criminal cases. Their work is to give a verdict; the word "verdict" is from the Latin *verumdictum,* a true sentence. And though they are under a necessity to bring in a verdict, yet they are in no snare to act against their consciences. If they are all of one mind, their way is fair; if they can't be all of one mind, they must, in civil cases, bring in for the defendant. In criminal cases they must bring in a "not guilty," for those are negative verdicts. The meaning is that they can't agree to give the case to the plaintiff or to condemn the prisoner. But these men may fail much when some, for quietness, comply with the judgment of others against their own light. So likewise, when they bring in a wrong verdict—whether from friendship, bribery, or credulity, depending on the infallibility of the lawyer who pleads the case—it would be very serviceable for these men to remember the judgment of the last day, and the punishment that will be inflicted on ungodly men. Under-officers may bring a woe upon themselves (Isaiah 10:1). Under-officers may prevent much injustice (John 7:46).

It would be a great benefit to buyers and sellers. There is an abundance of iniquity in sellers, such as when they sell that which is not worthy of being sold. Amos 8:6: "They sell the refuse of the wheat." They may take advantage of the ignorance and necessities of men to exact unreasonable prices from them, such as when they go beyond the bounds of truth in commending what they would sell, or when they do not tell of some defect in the product.

There is also an abundance of iniquity in buyers, when they run down the worth of what they would purchase by saying that they have bought the same thing much cheaper elsewhere, and saying that they will lose money if they buy this. Proverbs 20:14: " 'It is naught, it is naught,' saith the buyer; but when he goeth away, he boasteth." Some do not pay faithfully; sometimes they promise what they cannot see their way to perform.

Sometimes they neglect to pay when they could; because they can take advantage of their money, they defraud their creditors. Equivocation is interwoven in the very act of trading. If these men were afraid of hell, they would quickly leave off such methods. If they were sensible of what it is to be damned, they would not be so injurious to one another. They would remember that their gains will eat their flesh like fire (James 5:3).

It would be a great benefit to young persons. Many young persons take a licentious liberty. Some of them give way to a wanton spirit; they addict themselves to dalliance; they don't attend family orders, and spend the sabbath in a profane way. They are devoted to their pride, give themselves up to mirth and jollity, and neglect the opportunities of salvation.

The counsels of parents and warnings of teachers don't sink into their hearts. They hate to live a moping, melancholy life; they hate to be confessing their sins and crying to God for pardon. But if they were afraid of hell, that would make a mighty change in their carriage. A sense of hellfire would soon scare them out of those temperaments. They would not dare to do what now they are bold to do; they would have no heart to prosecute their carnal designs; they would be deaf to tempations; no arguments would prevail with them. They would as soon be persuaded to handle a burning-hot iron as to practice their former ways. They would soon be weaned from the world and take up the practice of religion. Ecclesiastes 11:9: "Rejoice, O young man in thy youth, and let thy heart cheer thee in the days of thy youth, and walk in the ways of thy heart, and in the sight of thine eyes; but know thou that for all these things God will bring thee into judgment."

USE 3. This is an exhortation to be afraid of hell. Man is a frightful creature, and is apt to be afraid of many little evils; yet, by reason of sin, men are so hard-hearted that they are not much afraid of hell. Christ Jesus directs us to be afraid of hell in Matthew 10:28: "Fear Him that can cast both body and soul into hell." Those especially who are in a natural state have reason to be afraid of hell. Isaiah 33:14: "Sinners in Zion are afraid, fearfulness hath surprised the hypocrites; who among us can dwell with everlasting burnings? Who among us can dwell with everlasting burnings?" Some men are much to blame that they put away the fear of hell; they shun and avoid it as best they can. But seriously consider whether you do not have abundant cause to fear hell. There are two things to be considered:

• First, the miseries of hell will be exceedingly great. The miseries that have been endured by some in this world have been amazing. It is hard to grapple with hearing of them, and it must be much harder to bear them; but the miseries of hell are far greater. Hebrews 10:31: "It is a fearful thing to fall into the hands of the living God." The apostle, speaking of the glory of heaven in 2 Corinthians 4:17, calls it "a far more exceeding and eternal weight of glory." So we may say of the misery of hell, it is a far more exceeding and eternal weight of misery.

Mind here these three things:

(1) The persons will be in distress; they rest not day or night. Their misery will be overbearing to them; there will be no room for any comforts; they will have no ease to comfort them; they will have no hopes to comfort them; they will have no peace of conscience to comfort them. They will wish they had not existed; they

will wish that they could cease to exist. Their former enjoyments will be no refreshment to them; their companions in misery will be no refreshment. They must endure suitable revenges for all their rebellions and the contempt that they have cast upon God. They will be standing monuments of the vengeance of heaven. Romans 2:8–9: "God will render indignation and wrath, tribulation and anguish." If their strength were the strength of stones or the flesh of brass, they could not endure their misery. They will have anguish of spirit, and will not know what in the world to do; there will be dreadful wailing (Matthew 13:42). They will lament their sins; they will bewail the loss of opportunities; they will condemn their folly; they will curse themselves; they will wish that they had never seen such things as their hearts now dote upon; their cry will go up to heaven; they will wish that they had no senses; their hearing, seeing, and feeling will be their misery, their misery their understanding, and their conscience their torment. They will wish that they had no bodies and no souls. Their bodies and souls will be vessels of wrath.

(2) These miseries are set forth by doleful comparisons. No comparison can fully set forth the miseries of hell because those miseries exceed all others. But some miseries may, in an effecting manner, represent to us something of the miseries of hell. Hell is compared to a dark dungeon (Matthew 8:12). The children of the kingdom shall be cast into outer darkness, so that in Jude 13 we read that "the blackness of darkness is reserved for ungodly men." The prophet Jeremiah was in a sorrowful condition when he was cast into the dungeon. It was a dark, miry hole, for "he sunk

in the mire" (Jeremiah 38:6). When persons are in a dungeon, they are confined and have no liberty; it is always dark and black night; they are cut off from all pleasant enjoyments; and they dwell in the shadow of death. A dungeon is next to a grave; there the light is as darkness.

Again, hell is compared to Sodom, when it was all on fire. Revelation 21:8: "They shall have their part in the lake that burneth with fire and brimstone, which is the second death." The people were in a miserable condition when streams of fire and brimstone fell from heaven upon their houses, their ground, and upon their bodies. Men, women, and children were all like torches: their bodies blazed, and how they screamed out and roared in that extremity! So hell is compared to the valley of the Son of Hinnom, where they burned their children to Molech. Hence hell is called "Gehenna," or the land of Hinnom (Matthew 5:29). So it is set forth by Tophet (Isaiah 30:33), which was the same place. There they burned children as sacrifices to the devil, and made a noise with trumpets and other instruments so that they might drown the noise of the cries of the poor children, for they could not bear their roarings. Hell is worse than all these.

(3) Whatever the miseries in hell are, they will be eternal. These miseries will never have an end. Life will have an end; this and that kingdom will have an end; the captivity of Babylon had an end; the rejection of the Jews will have an end; and the world will have an end. Matthew 25:46: "These shall go away into everlasting punishment." In Mark 9:44 the "worm dieth not," and there "the fire is not quenched."

The duration of their misery cannot be measured.

We may meaure the breadth of the earth and the circuit of the heavens, but we cannot measure eternity. Add thousands to thousands, and multiply millions by millions; fill quires of paper with numbers, and you can't measure eternity. It cannot be divided into days, years, or ages. Make ever so many parts of it, one will be eternal. When men have suffered never so long, there is an eternity remaining. It doesn't grow shorter and shorter. This makes every part of their misery infinite: their pain will be infinite and their terror will be infinite. If miseries could end, there would be an opportunity for comfort afterwards; but eternity cuts off opportunities for comfort. Men may well say, "Who can dwell with everlasting burnings?"

• Second, it is a difficult thing to escape hell. It may be avoided, and there are a number of men who do escape it, but they are few. It is a difficult thing to bear damnation, and a difficult thing to attain salvation. God has made a way of escape, but very few will comply with it. It is very cross to nature; it suits the glory of God, but it doesn't suit men's humours. Matthew 7:14: "Few there be that find it."

(1) Many who take pains to escape hell do not. Many men make attempts to escape it, but are not successful. Men are like prisoners who are bound with chains and cannot make their escape themselves. Many went out of Egypt who never reached Canaan. Some who endeavor to escape meet with disappointments and difficulties, and are discouraged. They are scared with the Anakims and high walls, and grow heartless. Some of them get into a wrong way; they get a dead faith and hope that will serve their turn. They have something like conversion, and take it for true conver-

sion. It passes with men, and they hope it will stand when they appear before God. They have gotten a righteousness, but it does not exceed the righteousness of the scribes and pharisees.

There are others who, after they have put away their sins and reformed their lives, return to their vomit again; some go on seeking till they are surprised by death. Death comes upon them before they have gotten through their work. There is a great difference between the number of those who seek and those who find. Luke 13:24: "Many seek, and are not able to enter."

(2) Many who think they have escaped will not. Men are ignorant, rash, and foolish, and so are not very capable of passing judgment on themselves. Their judgment is worth very little in a hundred other cases. But, indeed, wise men may easily be deceived, partly because of the similitude that is between false grace and true. I have read of a painter who pictured grapes so exactly that the birds were deceived and took them for real grapes. There is indeed a great difference between true grace and false; but there is also such a similitude that wise men may be mistaken. Men are frequently mistaken in silver and in jewels; so, if they look upon persons at a distance, they are easily mistaken in them. This is even more true when they look upon religious actions that have formerly been performed.

One great thing that exposes men to judge amiss is that they are prejudiced in one way or another; partly from pride, partly from fear, partly from love of ease, and partly from a dependence on the opinion of others. And for these reasons many are deceived. Proverbs 30:12: "There is a generation that are pure in their own eyes, yet are not cleansed from their filthiness."

Revelation 3:17: "Thou sayest thou art rich, and increased in goods, and hast need of nothing, and knowest not that thou art poor, and miserable, and wretched, and blind, and naked."

(3) Many whom the world blesses, as if they would escape, will not. Men are not competent judges of others. Men may have foundation enough for a judgment of charity, but they have no foundation for a judgment of certainty. Men may be very censorious of real saints, as Job's friends were; they may judge saints harshly because of their infirmities, and because of their own prejudices. So many have the reputation of saints who are not saints. Revelation 3:1: "Thou hast a name that thou livest, and art dead."

Men have nothing but external things to judge by which are separable from grace. Sometimes they take gifts for grace; but many have the gift of prayer who do not have the spirit of prayer. Sometimes men take common grace for special grace. Zeal and affection may be in men who are destitute of grace. Sometimes they take a religious conduct for a holy conduct. All that they judge by are only probable signs, and twenty probabilities will not make a thing certain. Probabilities may make a thing legal certain, but not infallibly so. Where there are only probabilities, there is a possibility of the contrary.

Many probabilities make a thing more probable, but they do not amount to a demonstration. Some of the wisest men have been mistaken: David was mistaken in the case of Ahithophel, the disciples in the case of Judas, and the church of Jerusalem with Nicholas of Antioch. No man can look into the heart of another and see there a spirit of love and faith. 1 Samuel 16:7:

"Man looketh on the outward appearance, but the Lord looketh on the heart."

Finis